The Accidental Drum Circle

A General Music Success Story

Mark Burrows

Editor: Kris Kropff
Cover Design and Illustrations: Jeff Richards
Book Design: Digital Dynamite, Inc.
Music Engraving: Linda Taylor
Dundun photo courtesy of Peripole™-Bergerault®, Inc. (www.peripolebergerault.com).
All other photos courtesy of Nina Burrows.

Heritage Music Press
A division of The Lorenz Corporation
P.O. Box 802
Dayton, OH 45401-0802
www.lorenz.com

Printed in the United States of America

ISBN: 978-0-89328-508-1

Dedicated to the outstanding students, teachers and staff of Stephen C. Foster Elementary School, Dallas

HMP
HERITAGE MUSIC PRESS
A Division of The Lorenz Corporation
Box 802 / Dayton, OH 45401-0802
www.lorenz.com

Contents

DAZED. CONFUSED. Overwhelmed.

hat pretty much describes my first experience as an elementary music teacher. I was fresh out of ollege with all kinds of great ideas and energy to burn. I had *no* idea what I was in for.

So you want me to teach where? In the auditorium? Okay. I can do that.

Oh, you need the auditorium this week for a book fair? I suppose I could teach in the foyer. Oh right, I forgot. That's where the students have art class. I guess I could teach outside. But what if it rai... Oh, never mind. I'll figure it out.

How much is the music budget?! I understand that the other teachers use a lot of their own money for supplies, but you see, I still have all these student loans...

You need me to play piano for the PTA program...tonight?! Actually, I was more of a vocalist in college. I barely made it out of class piano. Well, I'll see what I can do.

Sure. I'm happy to help out. Just one question——What exactly does a hall monitor do?

Sure. I'm happy to help out. Just one question——What exactly does a cafeteria monitor do?

Well, I suppose I could hold chorus rehearsals before school if that's the only time available.

Well, I suppose I could hold musical rehearsals after school if that's the only time available.

Another PTA program?! Didn't we just have one of those last month?!

Please don't misunderstand. I'm very grateful to get my first paycheck. I was just wondering who FICA is and why she gets so much of my money. You see, I still have all these student loans...

Somehow or another I managed to survive that first month. And once I started to figure things out and could catch my breath every now and then, I came to appreciate how lucky I was.

I was lucky to:
- Work with students who were bright, receptive and appreciative.
- Work alongside teachers who considered me a teammate, not merely a supporting character.
- Work for an administrator who valued the power of music and all fine arts in the education and emotional development of her students.

Even seemingly negative aspects had positive benefits.

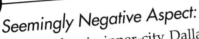

Seemingly Negative Aspect:
As a teacher in inner-city Dallas, my first "classroom" was the auditorium. (Actually, I was quite lucky to have an auditorium in which to teach. Many fellow music teachers didn't have a space nearly that permanent. They had to go from classroom to classroom using whatever materials they could fit on a cart (*music à la cart*).)

Positive Benefit:
My students were never intimidated about performing in the auditorium because that was their musical home.

Seemingly Negative Aspect:
Our school was overcrowded. With a student population over 1,200, the only way I could have every student in music at least once a week was to work with two classes at a time. It wasn't uncommon to have one class of children who spoke only English combined with one class of children who spoke only Spanish. Just imagine teaching four dozen five-year-olds for 45 minutes, where, no matter what you said, half the group had no idea what you were saying.

Positive Benefit:
I learned very quickly the importance of teaching by *showing* and *doing*, rather than *saying*.

Positive Benefit:
Music class became a safe haven for imagination, self-expression and plain old fun. Students looked forward to music even more during "Test Season." Even the classroom teachers got into the act, joining their students in music class to decompress and release some of that stress. Ironically, it was during these stressful times—where so much focus was placed on reading, writing and math—that the school community most appreciated the impact of music and all fine arts.

Seemingly Negative Aspect:
Standardized testing and test preparation are simply a way of life in public schools, from the district to the national level and all points in between. Administrators, teachers, students, and school staff feel the annual pressure to "get those scores up."

During my first spring as a music teacher, a series of very fortunate events began to unfold. Most of these events were not even of my doing, I more or less stumbled onto them. But, like pieces of a map, I was able to put just enough of them together to lead me to one of the coolest things I've ever been a part of—The Accidental Drum Circle.

THE DREADED DISCLAIMER

A familiar scene:

It's a weeknight. The kids are bathed, brushed, and in bed. (Finally!) I'm sitting on the sofa watching one of my favorite shows when a commercial comes on. This particular commercial is fast-paced with a series of very exciting images about a very exciting product. Accompanying these stirring visual images is the BIG VOICE. The BIG VOICE tells me all about the wonderful features of the product, and how my life won't be complete without it! The BIG VOICE tells me that this is the best product ever, and I'm convinced because the BIG VOICE sounds so excited. I can trust the BIG VOICE! The BIG VOICE is my friend!

Then comes the *super-fast-voice*. The *super-fast-voice* is trying to let me know that there are some exceptions to what the BIG VOICE told me. The *super-fast-voice* doesn't have much time to warn me because the BIG VOICE filled most of the commercial. The trouble is, I'm not even listening to the *super-fast-voice* because I'm still so caught up in the great sales job the BIG VOICE did. All I hear is "Blah-blah-blah…percent interest…yadda-yadda-yadda…offer invalid if…blah-blah-blah…may not be eligible."

Ah yes, the dreaded disclaimer. I've learned the hard way that those disclaimers can contain important information. I have a couple of disclaimers myself, which I'd like to share at the outset. Don't worry. No super-fast talking here.

Disclaimer #1:
I am **not** a professionally trained percussionist.

I taught music in the inner-city for several years. During that time I quickly discovered that students responded to percussion with unbridled enthusiasm. As a result, I tried to cultivate an environment where percussion, and drum circle in particular, could play a major role in the educational and emotional development of my students. Along the way I experienced amazing breakthroughs and colossal blunders, all of which I plan to share with you.

Disclaimer #2:
I am **not** a music therapist.

Drum circles have innumerable therapeutic benefits, from the release of stress to the building of self-esteem. I was able to share these and other benefits with my students, not because of any therapy expertise on my part, but simply because I was willing to provide opportunities.

Disclaimer #3:
This resource **is** geared towards the elementary music class.

There are many different kinds of drum circles, from community to high school to corporate to church to elementary school. *The Accidental Drum Circle* is a resource that may be useful for many of these different kinds of drum circles, but it is written from the perspective of an elementary music teacher. The activities and ideas presented are especially designed for students in second through sixth grade, and with a little tweaking, may be adapted for younger or older students.

You may have figured out by now why I've put the disclaimer at the front of this resource. From the outside looking in, drum circles can seem mysterious. And the drum circle facilitators can seem even more mysterious. The way they seem to bring so many people together into mesmerizing, pulsating rhythms while saying virtually nothing—surely they must hold some secret, some intangible quality bestowed upon only a few. Not true!

I was a music education major with a concentration in voice. Yet with no more than two hand-drum lessons to my credit, I put together a drum circle program that reached hundreds.

The bottom line is: If *I* can do it, *you* can do it!

THE WORLD'S SHORTEST GLOSSARY

ow many times have we been hesitant to try something new, not because the concepts involved were
that difficult to understand, but because the terminology was so confusing? How can we possibly
nderstand something new when the terms used to describe it are just as unfamiliar to us? Not to
orry, gentle reader. *The Accidental Drum Circle* is a resource written in plain English (and, at times,
ry poor English).

ith the exception of the names of a few instruments, there isn't much new lingo to learn. There are
vo terms, *facilitator* and *groove*, which are often used when discussing drum circle, and this resource is
o exception. So, without any further ado, I present the world's shortest glossary, made up of just two
rms (and like the disclaimer, I'm putting it out there right at the start).

Facilitator—one who makes easy

The role of the facilitator is to help the individuals realize their full expressive potential
while bringing those players together into one rhythmical, personal community. A good
facilitator steps in only when necessary and only when doing so adds to, rather than takes
away from, the creativity and expressiveness of the group.

ome will say that a facilitator is not there to teach. But this suggests that teaching only means stand-
ig at a chalkboard and lecturing for 45 minutes to a room full of students sitting dutifully in their
esks. Teaching can mean asking just the right question. Teaching can mean using eye contact, gesture
nd attentive listening to guide, rather than using words. Teaching can mean creating a welcoming
nvironment where self-discovery can take place. I believe that facilitation *is* a form of teaching, and a
eightened one at that.

Groove—the underlying pulse

The groove is a repeated rhythmic framework. Players each contribute their own rhythm
to the groove, creating a group rhythm. Once this group rhythm "locks," players can
vary individual rhythms, and even contribute solos. The groove is not so much a specific
rhythm as it is the *feel* of the music.

We interrupt this resource to bring you a painfully true story.

The Accidental Drum Circle

(OR: How great things kept falling in my lap and I nearly blew it anyway

I. A Lucky Break

It was the spring of my "rookie season" as a music teacher. The P.E. teacher had arranged for over 200 of our students to participate in a 5K run (walk) in downtown Dallas. Now get this—one of the sponsors of the event had issued an incentive that the school with the most participants would receive a very generous gift certificate for musical instruments. Guess which school had the most participants?

So, I headed down to the musical instrument dealer, loaded with purchasing power, ready to stock our music program with all kinds of instruments. I didn't exactly have a plan, just a vague sense that I should get some Orff instruments, and that kids really liked drums, so I should get some of those as well.

Learn from Mark's Mistake #1:

I had funds. I had enthusiasm. But I didn't have a plan. If I had thought about what the school really needed, and which instruments would have gotten the most use, I could have stretched my "drum dollars" a lot further. Some fairly expensive instruments sat on shelves, collecting dust, while others were in short supply. (The suggested collection of instruments on page 33 lists what I would buy now, having learned from my own mistake.)

What's a Drum Circle?

...er buying all the instruments I could with the gift certificate, I decided the school's instrument col-
...tion still needed a few hard-to-find instruments, such as the Australian didgeridoo. (Keep in mind
...s was in 1993. Didgeridoos are easier to come by these days.) I'd heard of this place up in Denton
...at sold instruments from around the world. I found what I was looking for, paid at the register, and
...s asked by the owner of the shop if I'd like to come back that night for drum circle. As usual, I had
...veral questions, including:

> What's a drum circle?

> When does it start, and how long does it last?

> Does it cost anything to participate?

> Do I need my own drum?

Doumbek

...e owner gave me a brief description of drum circle, including beginning
...d ending times. She said it didn't cost anything. She also assured me that
...didn't need my own drum, but if I'd like to purchase one, she had quite a
...ce selection. So I grabbed a quick bite and came back. And yes, I did buy
...drum—a ceramic doumbek. It is still one of my favorite instruments.

...he event started off slow as people came in from school, work or home and
...ined the circle. Within a half hour the circle of four had grown to nearly
...). Those that were there first had left lots of space for newcomers, but
...dn't hesitate at all to widen the circle even more whenever necessary.

...had seen a professional doumbek player before and remembered a few
...rokes, including a couple of fancy ones. Wanting to prove that I be-
...nged in the circle too, I started playing all these strokes, showing my
...ast knowledge" of an instrument I had just bought an hour earlier.

Learn from Mark's Mistake #2:

I was playing with my head, and not my heart. Have you ever been in a new situation where you
felt uncomfortable and, perhaps, a little inadequate? I think most students and teachers have, at
some point, heard that nagging inner-voice that says, "You can't do what they do. You really don't
belong here." Well, I gave that little voice too much attention and decided to battle it by showing
off. I didn't feel better. If anything, I felt worse, and a little embarrassed. I planned to leave once
the groove ended, but luckily there was an excellent facilitator on hand. During the groove, after
I'd stopped thinking about quarter notes and syncopated rhythms so much, I noticed that the facilitator was looking at my drum as I was playing. Then he looked me in the eye and smiled as if
to say, "That's it. I like what you're doing. It's good to have you in the circle." So I stayed.

Later, on the drive home, I thought about what had happened. I *did* belong in the circle. Not because I was an expert drummer (which, as you may recall, I am not), but because I was *me*. When
I stopped being myself I stopped giving the circle what I truly had to offer, and stopped receiving
all it had to give.

III. There's *Got* to Be a Way

For the rest of the spring and into the summer I began attending that same drum circle frequently. I even found where some other drum circles were being held to see how they did it. Some circles had facilitators while others seemed to be self-facilitated. Occasionally there would be the frustrated percussionist who wanted everyone to know that he was the "alpha drummer," but for the most part everyone was gracious, kind and inviting. I always came away from the drum circle experience feeling better and having learned something. All the while, I kept coming back to the thought, "There's *got* to be a way to do this in school."

The fall was going along pretty smoothly. I was now a second-year teacher, which meant I knew everything. One of my favorite activities was choir rehearsal, held every Tuesday and Friday morning at 7:30. Though this was 30 minutes before school began, there were always plenty of eager singers. On the way to choir rehearsal I always walked past the playground. It wasn't really on the way, but it helped me round up students and even do a little recruiting.

After a while I noticed that there were always about a dozen students sitting in "time out," already in trouble (usually for fighting) before the first bell. And it was quite often the same students. Too much unstructured time, I think. These students always got a stern talking-to from the assistant principal, and the multiple-repeat offenders were referred to the school counselor.

"There's *got* to be a way to do this in school."

One morning I visited the school counselor. I asked if she was seeing a lot of the same students before school. She said she was but, for reasons of privacy, couldn't give me names. So I made a decision. I told her that I would be available with the school's percussion instruments every Wednesday morning at 7:30 for students who would "rather beat on drums than on each other."

Learn from Mark's Mistake #3:

I tried to get a little too clever with the invitation. I went for a play on words that sent the wrong message. Drum circles can be a great way to relieve stress and express feelings, but it's never a good idea to *beat* a drum. Looking back, my invitation should have been for students who would "like to find healthy ways to express their feelings." Not as catchy, but more to the point.

Learn from Mark's Mistake #4:

In providing drum circle only for those who were encouraged to attend by the school counselor, I created a somewhat exclusive environment. The school had over 1,200 students, all of whom had needs, and all of whom could have benefited greatly from the drum circle experience. I would eventually remedy this situation, but it took a while.

IV. That First Wednesday Morning

I had no idea what to expect. I laid out about 25 different instruments (drums mostly) in the center of the floor. Then I waited. 7:30 came and went. Nobody yet. 7:40, still nobody. Then around 7:45 two boys came in together. They didn't know what to do, and I wasn't much help. I welcomed them and invited them to play any instruments they'd like. I told them I was there to help if they had any questions. Otherwise, they were free to do their own thing.

Slowly, tentatively, they started trying out various instruments. They headed for the large hand drums first. They played a while, got bored, then tried out the other percussion instruments, such as the guiro, shekeres, etc. When the 8:00 bell rang, they said "thanks" and left. I didn't know how to evaluate what had just happened. I felt disappointed that more students didn't come, but I was determined to give it a few weeks, and see what happened.

Learn from Mark's Mistake #5:

I should have provided more structure. If I had sat on the floor with a drum and started playing a simple groove, or even if I simply played a pop song on the radio, then at least there would have been a sense of rhythmic structure. The two boys would have then had the opportunity to participate in a group musical experience. Basically, what I had done was trade unstructured time with playground equipment for unstructured time with musical instruments. I forgot that it wasn't the drums those kids needed, but the circle.

V. Word of Mouth—
The Best Kind of Advertising

The following Wednesday morning I decided to set up everything as I had the previous week. It was 7:25 and I was about to sit and relax with my cup of coffee and five whole minutes of down-time, when I saw a head peek through the doorway. My two friends from the previous week, and they were early. Not only that, but they brought some friends, about five I think, four boys and one girl (bless her heart).

Word had gotten out that, if nothing else, there were some really cool instruments to play before school. The students didn't wait for an invitation, they just came in and started playing. The two boys from the previous week served as tour guides of sort, showing the others all the sounds the different instruments made and how to play them. I noticed that their technique wasn't bad at all, especially considering they had never played most of those instruments before.

No, I still didn't offer any structure, I just let them explore. Actually I'm very much in favor of giving kids a chance to explore, but without any structure, what I was providing wasn't really a drum circle experience, it was more like a percussion instrument petting zoo. It sounded a little like a zoo, too. But this morning did have a golden moment.

About halfway through the drum free-for-all, a couple of the students had gone to the side with their instruments and started playing a groove they heard on the radio the night before. I listened in as one student played the rhythm for the other. The second student had the idea to play a rhythm to complement the first rhythm. Honestly, it wasn't nearly that academic. It was more like, "Okay. You keep playing *that*, and I'll play *this*." They had created their own drum circle. They were playing together, listening to each other, cooperating, smiling, being their best selves. It even sounded cool—so cool that the other students started to notice and seemed interested in joining the groove. "Aha," I thought, "time for me to actually do something *useful*."

I invited everyone to bring an instrument and sit with me in a circle. I then asked the two-person drum circle to demonstrate the rhythm so we could all join in. They were more than happy to share the groove with everyone, and the circle grew from two to eight. No one tried to add a third rhythm. I think everyone was pleased that we were playing two parts at once, and it felt good. There was genuine energy in that group music-making experience—the kind of energy I had hoped for. If the 8:00 bell hadn't rung, we would have been there much longer. The students were excited, and energized for the day. Things seemed headed in the right direction.

You're probably looking for the "Learn from Mark's Mistake" segment, aren't you? I'm sure I made several mistakes, but hey, it was a good day!

VI. Forgetting the Circle

As the weeks went by, more and more students joined the drum circle. No longer were the participants just those who had been referred by the school counselor. There were boys and girls of all ages and personalities. We all found our comfort zone at about the same time. I became more comfortable as a facilitator and as a result the students became more open personally and musically. One could hear numerous rhythms within the same groove. I was struggling to get our school's choir singing in two parts, and here was this informal gathering of children, meeting once a week, playing four-, five-, even six-part percussion music.

This got me to thinking, "Wow, these kids sound great! I bet if we polish a couple of these rhythms, we could perform for PTA or an assembly and bring the house down!" And that's exactly what we did. Over the following weeks, the Wednesday-morning gatherings became rehearsals, drum circle grooves were considered little more than warm-ups for the actual percussion pieces. Fewer ideas came from the students, as I changed roles from facilitator to conductor.

The tangible result of this change was an amazing percussion ensemble. The group got so good that they performed at the Meyerson Symphony Center and on television. Corporations around the city brought in the percussion ensemble for entertainment. This was great! Right?

Learn from Mark's Mistake #6:

This was a *big* one—I forgot about the circle. I love ensemble playing and ensemble singing. Working with other musicians toward the common goal of a public performance can be an incredibly fun, educational and inspirational experience. As a percussion ensemble, the students were outstanding. The only problem is that a drum circle is not about performance.

Drum circle music should be spontaneous, inclusive, stress-free. Its purpose is immediate—connect people through a shared musical experience that builds community while celebrating individuality. By turning our drum circle into a performance ensemble with parts to learn, right and wrong rhythms, limited creative expression, and all-eyes-on-the-conductor admonishments, I took away the key to what made all the previous experiences so meaningful—the circle.

There was a place for a percussion ensemble at our school. I should have established a separate day, and possibly a different place for ensemble rehearsals. Then the drum circle could have continued to successfully fill the needs of students as only a drum circle could.

VII. Remembering the Circle

The negative effects of trading in drum circle for a percussion ensemble weren't obvious at first. Sure, we lost a few students along the way, mainly due to performance anxiety, but the performances themselves were wonderful. The percussion ensemble was always received by an enthusiastic audience. However, after providing entertaining concerts for over two years, the percussion ensemble started to lose ground.

Many of the players were tired of rehearsals, which were no longer quite as satisfying since they were always focused on upcoming performances. Some of the same students who had been referred to drum circle by the counselor were back on the playground before school, and, occasionally back in time out. It was time to do what I should have done in the first place.

I started holding drum circles *during* school hours, *during* music class time. Not every time. There was still the little matter of teaching notes, rhythms, singing, Beethoven's favorite snack,[1] and all. But occasionally the students, from kindergartners to fifth graders, would walk in to music class and see the percussion instruments in the center of the room, just waiting for eager little hands. The circle was back, and this time it was for everyone.

We now return you to your regularly scheduled resource.

---

[1] Mac 'n Cheese

The POWER of the Drum Circle Experience

Not too long ago I stumbled upon a quote by the great English composer Benjamin Britten:

> Any musical experience requires three people – composer, performer, listener. Without the presence of all three, there is no musical experience.

One of the unique aspects of drum circle is that you get to be all three of these people at once. The circle creates the music, the circle plays the music, and the circle listens to the music. What a rewarding, fulfilling experience!

Another aspect that makes the drum circle experience so powerful is its inclusiveness. Imagine making music with a group of people where no audition is needed and you are accepted just as you are. In fact, the one thing the circle wants and needs is for you to be yourself.

The drum circle experience is also one that is accessible. One doesn't need years of lessons to produce a sound on a drum. True, there are master drummers who spend their whole lives learning to play highly sophisticated rhythms. But virtually no technical know-how is necessary to have a successful drum circle experience.

WHY A CIRCLE?

For those of us who are used to standing in front and conducting a choir or instructing from a chalk board, the circle will take a little getting used to. Remember, it's called drum *circle*, not circle *drumming*.

Here are some reasons why the circle is so vital:

- It offers a sense of *equality*. There is no front or back. No first or last. We are all equal.
- It offers a sense of *community*. We sit or stand side by side and see each other face to face. Everyone has a place in the circle.
- It offers a sense of *connection with world cultures*, who traditionally gather in a circle for music-making. This may be a big reason why percussion instruments from around the world fit so well with drum circles. These instruments seem to reflect the global nature of the drum circle.
- It lessens the need for *discipline*, especially with younger students. Because there is no front or back, there is no back row. In everyday music class, how often have you had to discipline students in the front row? The back row?
- It offers a safe environment for *peer-to-peer learning*. Young people are very strongly influenced by their peers. Drum circle allows peers to share with one another, and learn from one another, in a safe environment where *you* set the parameters.

HOW TO CIRCLE

There are many great reasons for establishing the circle. And there are many ways to set up a circle. In elementary music class, where students typically cannot bring their own instruments, here's one way that works.

1. Before the students arrive, place the instruments, along with all necessary mallets, in the center of the room (or whatever the music space happens to be). This helps establish a center or focal point of the circle that isn't the facilitator.

2. Place chairs around the room in a circle wide enough for students to enter and sit. If you teach in a multi-purpose room where chairs for all students aren't available, the students can sit or stand in a circle. Younger students are used to sitting "criss-cross applesauce," but older students, with longer legs, will need to stand from time to time. Also, a few chairs will be needed for those playing large hand drums. The advantages of chairs are that they tend to be more comfortable and they allow you to design the circle in advance. Often a student-formed circle will have gaps or corners that need to be adjusted.

3. If you have more students than will fit in one circle around the room, have two (or more) concentric circles. This is not the ideal, but may be the only practical way to seat a large group. If you know in advance that you will have a large group, have the concentric circles set up in advance. This will save hurt feelings later on since you won't need to tell some students to form an "outer circle." Make sure there are several people in both circles so that no one feels like an outsider.

4. As the students enter, have them sit in the chairs, or form their own circle around the instruments. Some students will be too tempted and will play a drum on their way to a chair. It happens. Kindly ask them to stay in the circle and wait until it's time to choose an instrument. (This way differs from some community drum circles. In those circles people may bring their own drums, or calmly walk to an instrument which has been placed by, on, or in front of a chair, and join in the rhythm. If you want to see all-out mayhem, tell two dozen first-graders who have just entered the music room to go pick an instrument. See if any of them actually hear you when you shout, "No, don't run! Remember to share! Wait, Maria had that first! Everyone will get to play the djembe eventually!")

Djembe

5. Once the students are in a circle, invite small groups to choose instruments and take them back to the circle. Try to make the groupings arbitrary, such as, "All those with red shoes may go choose an instrument." Assure those who choose last that there will be plenty of opportunities to exchange instruments. You may need to help some of the younger students take their instrument choices (a large conga, for example) back to the circle. If you have concentric circles, make sure there is enough space for students in the wider circle to enter the center of the room and return to the circle with their instrument choice.

6. Through the course of the drum circle, have the students exchange instruments. You may need to help facilitate amicable exchanges. A good way to do this is to have the students put the instruments down and move three spaces to the left.

7. After the drum circle time has come to a close, choose arbitrary groups to take the instruments back to the center of the circle, then line up (back to lines so soon?) at the door.

First, Do No Harm:
Some hand-drumming basics

Imagine being a kid. (Come on, we're music teachers; this shouldn't be much of a stretch.) It's your fir[st] day of soccer practice. You have on your new cleats. The ride in the backseat seems to take forever. Yo[u] can't wait to get on that field with all your friends and start scoring goals! Then, when you get there, [a] brand new soccer ball waiting in plain sight, the coach has all the players "take a knee" as he goes ov[er] all the Dos and Don'ts (mostly Don'ts) of soccer. Twenty deflating minutes later, you and the rest [of] your rule-weary teammates take the practice field, no longer playing, but constantly wondering, "A[m] I doing this right?"

If students are coming to you knowing there's a chance to play percussion instruments, they're goin[g] to be excited. In other words, momentum is building before a single student enters the room. It's im[-] portant to keep this momentum going by having the students play as soon as possible. Most of the Do[s] and Don'ts (mostly Dos) can be taught during the course of playing through good modeling on you[r] part, or the occasional mini-lesson between grooves. There are, however, a few things the student[s] need to be aware of from the get-go. Most of these are related to health and safety.

- First, do no harm. Music shouldn't hurt. *Play* drums, don't *beat* them. I've always told drum circle participants, "Drum sticks and drum heads can be replaced. Your fingers and hands cannot. Play with respect for the instruments and respect for yourselves."
- Remind students to remove rings and bracelets before playing.
- Encourage students to be mindful of the volume level. "When we play from the heart, we show respect for ourselves. When we play softly enough to hear someone else play from his heart, we show respect for each other."
- If you have all the instruments set out in the center of the floor with the intent that the students will walk in and each go to an instrument, make sure they walk. Assure them that players will trade instruments often so that each student will, at some point, get to play her favorite. As a facilitator, make sure to rotate instruments between grooves.

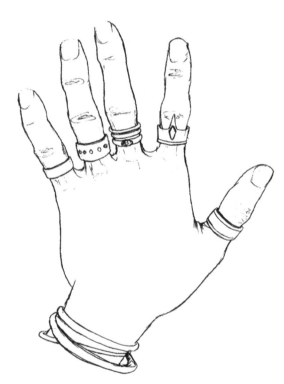

Remind students to remove rings and bracelets before playing!

Most of the other basics can be taught or, even better, modeled during play. Many of these basics rei[n]force proper drumming technique.

Hand-Drumming Basics:

The Bounce
The hand should bounce off the drum head, rather than stick to it, to let the instrument vibrate.

Bass and Tone
There are two basic sounds for most hand drums. Actually, there are tons of different sounds, but for our purposes we'll focus on the two primary ones. The *bass* is produced by bouncing the hand (fingers together) in the center of the drum head. The *tone* is produced by bouncing the pads of the fingers (fingers together) near the rim.

Play from the elbow, not the wrist.

The Mallet Grip
Hold the mallet with all the fingers wrapped around the stick. Mallets should also bounce.

Relax
Tension has a tendency to creep into the shoulders and neck. If you see a player with neck or shoulder tension, roll your own shoulders and gently move your head from side to side, as if releasing your own tension. Stretching, like yawning, is contagious. Most students, upon seeing you stretch to relax, will do the same, often without realizing it. And breathe. A lot of tension occurs when players don't breathe deeply, or hold their breath too much.

Positioning the Instrument
For a drum with one head, such as a conga, djembe, etc., make sure the open end is not covered so that the drum can resonate. For larger hand drums, sit in a chair and slightly tilt the drum forward. This can be tricky for smaller players. A few drum stands can be a worthwhile investment. Also, make sure open ends of drums (or any other instruments for that matter) are not aimed at another player's ears. Ouch!

All of these basics, once learned, will help maximize the playing experience. And while these basics are important, it is also important to allow the students a chance to "discover" the instruments and themselves. If a student has found a unique way to play an instrument that is safe and healthy for player and instrument, fine. Proper technique will come.

Whenever possible, teach by showing rather than saying. If one or two students are having difficulty, don't feel the need to bring the groove to a grinding halt. Simply demonstrate as inconspicuously as possible.

From time to time you may need to reinforce a concept verbally. That's okay. Rely on your Music Teacher super power of observation to determine when a mini-lesson on technique might be in order. Before the next groove, simply go over the basic (or basics) that needs a little attention. A good way to reinforce basics without losing momentum is to play an echo game. "Everyone look and listen. Echo the rhythm I play while imitating the way I play it." Now you're helping the students improve a skill while disarming any of their defensiveness, because they're having fun!

Here's a short list of priorities I like to keep in mind. It is helpful when determining what needs to be said at the outset, what can be shown while playing, and what can be emphasized as part of a mini-lesson.

1. Look after the physical, mental, and emotional well-being of all the people (this includes you).

2. Foster an environment of respect for each other.

3. Foster an environment of respect for the instruments.

4. Set a tone that is fun, spontaneous, inclusive, and non-judgmental.

5. Demonstrate active listening skills.

6. Demonstrate a few basic techniques.

7. Demonstrate a few basic rhythms.

But what about focusing on a good sound and tight ensemble playing? Those are excellent goals for a *percussion ensemble*. Remember, the focus of the drum circle should be on the *circle*.

Putting on the Facilitator's Hat

After reading the story of my Accidental Drum Circle, complete with all (most (well, several)) of my mistakes, you may be wondering, "Gee, Mark, did you do *anything* right?" I will answer that question by saying that I did just enough right to keep it going. (And yes, I'm just as surprised as you are that despite all my mishaps, I was still asked to write this resource.)

I've since facilitated numerous drum circles for children, adults and multigenerational groups. (My facilitation skills are showing real signs of improvement.) Still, if you've read the last 18 pages, you know better than to follow my example. So allow me to share with you, from the perspective of a drum circle player, traits that I have most valued in facilitators.

I appreciate a facilitator who is:

 Inviting. We all need to feel that we belong. The facilitator doesn't have to do much. A kind, welcoming word or a smile can make a big difference.

 Nonjudgmental. Nobody wants to "mess up," especially in public. The facilitator has the ability to create a safe environment with no "wrong" rhythms.

 A good listener. When a facilitator truly listens, he gives the drum circle and its individual members the knowledge that they are being heard—that they, and what they play, matter. A good listener can hear when a groove is winding down and be prepared to facilitate another groove, or bring the circle to a close. A good listener also knows when to be more active in helping others.

 Energetic, yet relaxed. I love playing in a drum circle with an energetic facilitator. One of the best things a facilitator can be is a model for positive energy and a positive attitude. That energy is most effective when balanced with a relaxed attitude that puts the players at ease.

 Adept at teaching by showing and doing rather than saying. As a drum circle participant I've always learned most effectively when I was shown how to do something during the course of play. When a facilitator can teach by showing and doing, she can offer help in an inconspicuous way that doesn't place any unwanted attention on an individual.

Clear and succinct when speaking. There are times, especially with younger players, when teaching by saying will be necessary. A facilitator might wish to demonstrate a new rhythm or simply offer positive feedback to the drum circle. A facilitator should keep comments brief for a couple of reasons. First of all, more talking means less playing, and people are there to play. Secondly, the players are holding instruments. They can hold those instruments and listen to a facilitator for only so long before their hands (involuntarily or not) start playing.

 Helpful. There are times in a drum circle when I have a hard time getting in the groove. Often, I like to work it out on my own, finding just the right rhythm for the circle and myself. Other times it's nice to know that there is an attentive facilitator who can help reconnect me, rhythmically or otherwise, to the circle.

 Genuine. I can most easily be myself in a drum circle when I see the facilitator being himself. When the facilitator puts on a persona and "plays to the crowd," members of the circle may be entertained, but they may also begin to feel like an audience. Facilitators come in all types—funny, mellow, exuberant, soft-spoken. The facilitator who is true to herself sends a message that the circle is an open place where you are welcome just as you are.

 Encouraging. Whether at work or at play, we all want to feel successful. And most players, no matter how confident, will still look to the facilitator for assurance. Once again, a smile, a kind word, or even a simple "thumbs up" can be a huge difference-maker.

 Organized. The success of a spontaneous music-making experience depends on a facilitator who is organized. The facilitator should have instruments (with sticks, if required) in place before the first person walks in. If one groove winds down and a new one doesn't emerge from within the circle, the facilitator should be prepared with a rhythm. A good facilitator reminds me of a swan—smooth and effortless on the surface, but just underneath the surface, paddling like crazy.

 Part of the circle. I really admire the facilitators who, rather than standing in the center, join the rest of us in the circle. Sure, they may move from place to place on occasion, or stand to say a word or two. But when the facilitator sits with the circle, he embodies some of the best ideals of the circle: We are in this together. We are all equal. Your ideas are just as valid as my ideas.

You may have noticed that the list does *not* contain anything about the facilitator needing to be an excellent percussionist.

Sometimes They Just Need You to Listen...

My wife comes home from work one day. She's physically and emotionally drained. It's one of those if-anything-can-go-wrong-it-will kind of days. She collapses in a chair in the living room and proceeds to tell me all about it. About halfway through, I interrupt with words to the effect of, "Here's what you should do." I then give her what I consider to be the perfect solution to her problem.

Long silence follows. (The silence is long enough for me to notice, so we're talking *looooong*.)

My wife looks me in the eye and says, more patiently than I deserve, "Honey, I don't need you to *fix* my problem for me. I just need you to *listen*."

As a facilitator, one of the best ways to support the drum circle is by listening.

But what if the playing gets faster and faster?

Let it. The circle might recognize what is happening and make an effort to steady the group tempo. Or the circle will play faster and faster until it can no longer keep up, and the groove will collapse on itself. The circle has just *experienced* what happens when the tempo gets too fast. The facilitator doesn't have to say anything. He could, however, ask a couple of follow-up questions, "What happened?" "What could we do differently next time?"

But what if the playing gets slower and slower?

Let it. The circle might recognize what is happening and make an effort to steady the group tempo. Or the circle will play slower and slower until it fizzles out completely. The circle has just *experienced* what happens when the tempo gets too slow. The facilitator doesn't have to say anything, or she could ask follow-up questions that allow the circle to come up with solutions. Sometimes the circle will play slower and slower because the current groove has lost some of its allure. After the groove has fizzled out, invite the circle to start a new one.

By allowing the groove to speed up or slow down to the point that the players can't maintain the pulse, the student will have taught themselves a valuable lesson on maintaining the pulse. If you absolutely can't take it, you can use an easy-to-hear instrument, such as a cowbell, and play a steady pulse that brings the circle back to a manageable group tempo.

But what if the playing gets louder and louder?

Unlike playing too slow or too fast, playing too loud can have negative physical side effects. It can be rough on the ears, rough on the hands and fingers, and rough on the instruments. The facilitator must always put the well-being of the members of the circle above all else.

If the playing is way too loud, don't hesitate to stop the groove and remind everyone of the drum circle basics. But if the playing is just a little louder (or softer, or busier, etc.) than it ought to be, there are some nonverbal ways to communicate with the players while allowing them to continue playing.

The facilitator can help the drum circle along by *listening* rather than *fixing*, provided that a very special kind of listening takes place...

(((Active Listening)))

Active listening allows the listener to communicate, often nonverbally, with the speaker.

Why is active listening so important?

- It validates others and their points of view.
- It keeps the lines of communication open.
- It helps to avoid misunderstandings.
- It opens up people to new ideas and to each other.

In the above question, if I had replaced "active listening" with "drum circle" I could have easily come up with the same answers. Active listening is one of those incredibly valuable *life* skills, which happens to also have amazing benefits in the drum circle.

The following are a few active listening skills, with ideas for applying them in a drum circle setting.

Eye Contact

This is a big one. Make eye contact with every member of the drum circle as often as possible. Establishing good, consistent eye contact makes it easier to give non-verbal cues. Eye contact also sends the affirming message to each member of the circle that, "I see *you*. I recognize what you bring to the circle. You are a vital part of this group."

Face the Person

This is easy in a one-on-one conversation, but how do you face an entire drum circle at once? Personally, I prefer to sit with the circle rather than stand in the center of it. I tried standing in the center a few times, but I always had my back turned to someone. Sitting with the circle allows me to face everyone, plus it takes some of the focus off the facilitator and puts it where it belongs—on the shared musical experience. It's a good idea to mix it up by moving to different parts of the circle.

Occasionally the only way all the players can fit into a space is by forming concentric circles. Only then will I stand in the center, turning to face each player as often as possible.

Don't Interrupt

Whenever possible, try to guide the circle without stopping to give verbal instructions. If the playing gets a little too loud, hold out your hand, palm down, and lower your hand until the volume is at an acceptable (healthy) level. Or simply point to your own ears, reminding the players to listen to themselves. They will usually adjust the sound accordingly.

Suspend Initial Judgment

Sometimes a groove takes a while to get going. Rather than stopping and starting over with "something better," allow the players enough time to express, explore and experience. Trust that the healthy group dynamic you've helped establish can lead to an excellent musical experience—it may just need a little time to get where it's going.

Relax

All of the active listening skills listed above work best when you are relaxed. For example, forceful eye contact can be intimidating and shut down the line of communication before it really develops.

When you facilitate by actively listening rather than fixing, you validate the ideas generated by the players while empowering the circle with a healthy sense of self-esteem and self-reliance.

Getting in the Groove

Another familiar scene:

It's an elementary school classroom. The teacher hands out sheets of white and assorted-color paper to all the students and says, "Make a picture." Sure, a couple of students start to color almost immediately, but most are frozen. "Make a picture of *what*?" A little too much creative freedom, perhaps? Give those same students even the slightest guidance…

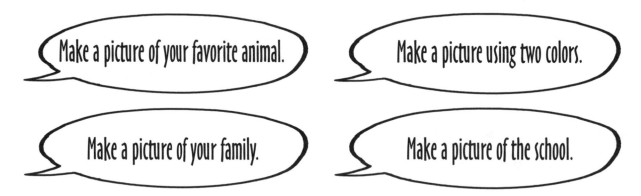

Make a picture of your favorite animal.

Make a picture using two colors.

Make a picture of your family.

Make a picture of the school.

…and watch them go! Sometimes it just takes that little spark.

(I drew my family *with* my favorite animals. . .

he same is true with drum circle.

groove can occur spontaneously from within the circle with no prompting on the part of the facilita-
r. This happens fairly often, but not always. The facilitator needs to be ready to help get the circle in
ie groove. Here are a few ideas:

- Play a CD of popular music (check the lyrics first) or world drumming as the students enter. As the CD continues to play, give each student an instrument. The students will usually start play-ing along with the CD. If not, invite them to do so. As the students get into the groove, gradually fade out the CD and allow the circle to continue playing.
- Invite the students to play the rhythms of their names over and over. (See below for some ex-amples.) Encourage the students to play softly as they find how to contribute their individual name rhythms to the group rhythm. Gradually, a groove should form. Give it time.

- Have the students sing a song they all know. Invite them to create a groove based on the rhythm of the words to that song.
- Try some of the "conversation starters" offered below. They are simple rhythms that can be used to spark a new groove.

Mixing it Up

Keeping the *groove* from becoming a *rut*

Sometimes a groove will get going and no one really wants to stop. Everyone is locked in to the puls with their own unique rhythm. Students are playing without over-thinking. What an experience! Oth times, it can seem like a rut. "We just keep playing the same thing over and over?! That doesn't sound lik much fun to me. It sounds kind of boring." Keeping the drum circle fresh, yet natural can be a challeng Here are some ways to mix it up.

Create a dynamic landscape.

Once a groove establishes itself, take the circle through loud and soft sections. Have the players watch and respond as you raise your hand, palm up, to indicate louder, and lower your hand, palm down, to indicate softer. Better yet, invite a member of the circle to indicate louder and softer sections. Make sure to choose a student who is comfortable with this.

Play something in free rhythm.

Invite each player to contribute a sound or rhythm to a group soundscape.

Tone Color

Have an instrument group play the groove while other instrument groups listen. Some instrument groupings include all the hand drums, all the shakers, all the wood-sounding instruments, etc. The trick here is in how to cue in all the players without disrupting the flow of the groove. One way is to point to your eyes as a signal for everyone to watch. Then point to an instrument (not the player of that instrument). All the players with similar instruments should continue in the groove while the others stop and listen. Do this for all the instrument groupings. Indicate for everyone to play by making a horizontal circular motion with one hand. By the way, it's best to have a mini-lesson on cueing before trying it in a groove. The students will watch for signals, but they still need to know what the signals mean. Two quick things about cueing: always be clear and always be consistent. Once you've established that a certain signal means something, don't change the meaning midstream.

Rumble

This works well near the close of a groove. Hold out your hands, fingers spread, and shake your hands. This indicates students should play a "rumble" on their instruments—drum rolls, shake rattles, etc. End the rumble with everyone playing one strong beat. Prepare the circle for the strong final beat by lifting the hands up (the upbeat, or prep). Then, bring them down to indicate a group strong beat (downbeat). Once you have demonstrated how to do this, allow students to guide a rumble and strong-beat finish.

There are also some fun rhythm games which can be played between grooves. These games can help spark rhythmic creativity later on in another groove.

- **The Echo Game.** Play a simple rhythm and have the students echo. Allow each student an opportunity to play a rhythm to be echoed. Likewise, allow a student to say, "No thank you." The students learn how to reproduce a rhythm they hear, as well as create a new one.
- **Call and Response Game.** This game is a little different than the Echo Game. Play a 4-beat call and have the students play a set response. (See example below.) Then play a different 4-beat call and have the students give the same response. Allow each student an opportunity to play a call. Like the echo game, students are reproducing a rhythm (this time, repeatedly) and creating a new one, but here they are also learning the call and response form, which is important in world music as well as Western art music.

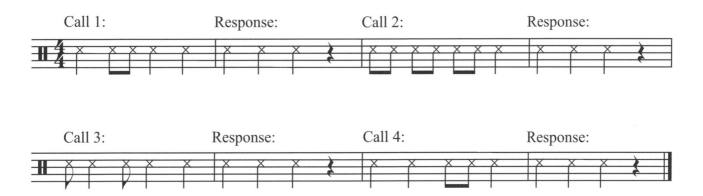

- **Pass the Beat.** Sit with the students in the circle. Establish a steady beat in $\frac{4}{4}$ time. Play beat 1. Have the student to your right play beat 2. The student to his or her right plays beat 3, and so on. Each student plays one beat, passing it around the circle. The students learn how to keep a steady beat, and internalize the pulse.
- **The Name Game.** Sit with the students in the circle. Say your name as you play the rhythm of your name on an instrument. (See page 27 for a few examples.) Go around the circle, inviting each student to say and play his or her name. This game can be played with other things besides names—favorite flavor of ice cream, favorite animal, or a dream job. The students learn to look for rhythms in the world around them. They also learn about each other.

YOU DON'T HAVE TO PLAY IT ALL:
THE ART OF LEAVING SPACE

Some drum circle participants, especially at first, will hear an involved rhythm and try to play the whole rhythm alone. It's hard to blame them, really. Mention the word "drumming" and many of us think about the drummer in a rock band who plays all those drums and cymbals by herself.

I encourage players to think of a drum circle groove as a group mural. Each individual contributes something to the big picture, and leaves space for everyone else to do the same.

The following is a sample rhythm which can seem busy if played by one person.

And here is that same rhythm divided between two players. Each player contributes a distinct rhythm that allows space for the other. The two more spacious rhythms fit together to form a new, shared rhythm.

If several players seem to be trying to do too much, model spacious playing yourself.

Special Concerns

Even the smoothest sailing can be interrupted by choppy waters. The following are a few special concerns and what the facilitator can do to help.

A student just doesn't have rhythm.

The student who doesn't have a sense of rhythm is *incredibly* rare. Rhythm can be a very abstract concept, but it doesn't need to be. Help this student by having him watch as you play a simple rhythm along with the groove. Invite that student to play with you based on what he sees. Or, direct his attention to the instrument of another student who is locked in the groove. Perhaps, have people change places between grooves and guide the student having difficulty to a spot near a student who is more comfortable. If all else fails, give this student an instrument, such as a rainstick, where specific rhythm isn't necessary.

A student is a natural at drumming...

...and wants everyone to know it. Is this student showing off or expressing her deepest feeling through music? It's hard to tell. The best thing is to allow this student time and space to play, then acknowledge her with an affirming smile or "thumbs up." That is usually all the student is looking for, anyway—affirmation. If the soloing persists, wait until the drum circle time is over and discreetly remind this student that it's okay to play a solo, but that it is important to leave space for others, too.

No place in the groove

A student has a hard time finding his place in the groove. This can happen even when the student has a strong sense of rhythm. Sometimes the groove generated by the circle simply doesn't "speak" to everybody. Encourage this student to join in by playing to the steady beat.

An obscured groove

Sometimes, the groove is blurry to the point that it isn't much of a groove at all. This is usually the result of students trying to play too much. Look to the hand drums first. Most of these can be played by two hands at once, making it possible to play busier rhythms. Remind students that they don't have to do it all by demonstrating a more open rhythm that leaves space.

The groove seems a little too sparse

This is usually a result of many players playing the same rhythm. They are all leaving space, but in exactly the same places.

Invite some players to fill in the open spaces by demonstrating on your own instrument. The following is an example of how to play in the spaces.

The circle seems to be losing energy

The players may be tired. They may also be tired of the current groove. Be ready to bring the groove to a close and play a rhythm game, or spark a new groove. By the way, don't be in a hurry to bring a still-strong groove to a close, even if it's been going for a while. Some grooves last longer than others. There's very little that feels better than a groove where everyone is locked in.

Adding Spice to Your Circle

You know how the old saying goes—variety is the spice of life. The same is true for drum circles. Try to provide the widest variety of percussion instruments possible. This includes variety in:

- **Kinds of instruments**, such as hand drums, drums played with sticks, rattles, bells, tambourines, instruments to be scraped, rhythm sticks, and so on.
- **Tones**, from deep bass drums to high-pitched bells and everything in between.
- **Cultures represented**, such as Brazilian, West African and Native American. Virtually every culture on the planet has some kind of percussion instrument that can enhance the drum circle experience.

Just like spices, tastes in instruments vary greatly. If I had to start from scratch, here's how I would stock the school's musical "spice rack."

Dundun   Taos Drum

Ashiko   Djembe

Caxixi   Shekere

Doumbek   Bodhran

1. Some kind of bass drum, such as the Brazilian *surdo*, West African *dundun*, or large Taos drum. Every drum circle needs a heartbeat, and the bass drum provides it. It only takes one to anchor a smaller drum circle. But as the circle reaches twenty or more players, consider adding another bass drum of some kind.

2. A few large hand drums, such as the West African *djembe* and *ashiko*, or the Cuban *congas*. Let's face it, it's called "drum circle" for a reason. Large hand drums are gratifying to play and visually appealing. Because these instruments are played with both hands, they can be used for busier parts. Therefore it doesn't take but a few large hand drums to work effectively. In fact, too many of these drums played at once can sound blurry. One of these drums, if struck in the center of the drum head, can serve as the bass drum.

3. Several different kinds of rattles, such as the Latin American *maracas*, the Brazilian *caxixi*, or the West African *shekere*. Rattles are great for keeping the steady beat or filling in the spaces left by the bass drums. Rattles are also great "entry" instruments for those who may yet be a little self-conscious for the big drums and solo instruments. Most rattles are relatively inexpensive, making it easy to acquire rattles from many world cultures. It's fun to see how different cultures make rattles using whatever materials are readily available.

4. A few small hand drums and frame drums, such as the Middle Eastern *doumbek*, the Irish *bodhran*, the Cuban *bongos*, or the Brazilian *tambourim*. These instruments are great for reinforcing the pulse. They can also provide solo opportunities.

5. Wooden sticks, such as rhythm sticks, Hawaiian *puili sticks*, or Cuban *claves*. These instruments are great for supporting the steady beat or the backbeat (beats 2 and 4 in a $\frac{4}{4}$ groove). Claves even have their own characteristic rhythms which are practically synonymous with Cuban dance music.

6. A few tambourines. These are great for reinforcing the steady beat, playing on the backbeat, or even subdividing the steady beat.

7. Bells, such as the West African *gankogui*, Brazilian *agogo bells*, or a simple cowbell. These are great for playing more syncopated rhythms. One or two sets at most will be plenty. These are very loud instruments that can be easily heard over everything else.

8. A sound-effect instrument or two, such as the Andean *rainstick* or the ocean drum. These instruments produce unique sounds, and are great for those players who find steady rhythms difficult to play.

Claves

Agogo Bells

Rainstick

Ocean Drum

A collection like this would be a great start. Of course, there are literally thousands more percussion instruments, each offering their own unique flavor. Here are a couple of favorites:

- *Cuica.* This is a friction drum from Brazil. The player uses a damp cloth to rub a stick embedded in the drum head. The cuica can, among other things, imitate animal sounds.
- *Talking Drum.* This drum is shaped like an hourglass. The player holds the drum under one arm and squeezes a series of threads while striking the drumhead with a beater in the other hand. This squeezing and relaxing causes the drum head to tighten or loosen, which raises or lowers the pitch. In West Africa, the talking drum is considered a long-range communication device as much as a musical instrument.

Has the following thought just crossed your mind? "That's great, Mark. All those instruments from all over the world sound very exciting. I'm sure my students would love to play every one of them. But how much is all this going to cost?!"

Perhaps there's a school district out there willing to heap thousands of dollars upon its elementary music program (and if there is, I'm moving there). But the reality is that most of us have very limited funds to spend on our music programs. Once we've purchased a new song book or two, a new holiday musical, a decent recording of *Peter and the Wolf,* and the basics like chalk, erasers, pencils, staff paper, etc., we have precious little left to spend on musical instruments.

First of all, let me say that, compared to most instruments, multicultural percussion instruments are quite reasonable. As an experiment, I went out with $300 of my own money to assemble a collection of multicultural percussion instruments. I was able to get everything pictured on the opposite page.[1]

This collection came from a variety of sources, including musical instrument dealers, import stores and the internet. I could have a built a much larger collection of instruments, but would have sacrificed

---

[1] Now, that's $300 as of 2006, the year this resource was first published. If you're reading this book in the year 2056 A.D., you may have to spend a little bit more.

quality in the process. Import stores often carry unique instruments not carried by musical instrument dealers. Be careful, however, as some of these instruments are really intended as decoration and aren't made out of the best materials. It's wonderful to have lots of instruments that look, feel and sound authentic. On the other hand, a question you should always ask yourself when evaluating an instrument for drum circle is, "Will this instrument hold up after years of use by elementary school children?"

Secondly, don't feel that you have to get all the instruments at one time. Building a fine collection of *anything* takes time. The same is true with percussion instruments. Get what you can when you can. The rest can wait until next year's budget.

Thirdly, and most importantly, remember that the most important word in drum circle isn't drum, it's *circle*. You don't need a lot of drums, rattles, bells, and whistles to have an incredibly rewarding group music experience. If you have a circle of enthusiastic students, then you're ready to go!

1. Djembe
2. Murgu drum (East African hand drum)
3. Wooden frame drum
4. Gankogui
5. Shakere
6. Guiro
7. Tambourine
8. Rainstick
9. Caxixi
10. Chajes (Andean goat-top rattle)
11. Frog rasp
12. Native-American rattle

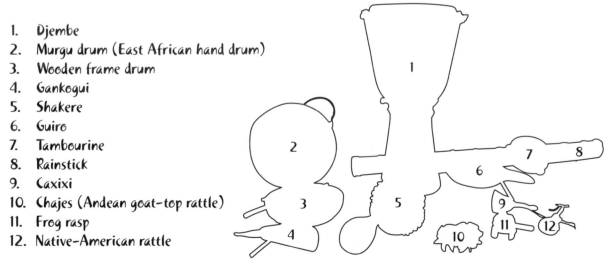

Drum Circle Without Drums

Here are a few ways to have a great music circle experience when you don't have enough drums to go around, or simply don't have drums at all.

Body Percussion

This is a great option even if you have tons of percussion instruments. There are many cultures throughout the world that, despite having musical instruments available, prefer to use body percussion. Body percussion stimulates movement and helps players to better internalize rhythms, and each player can produce more sounds than all the world's percussion instruments combined.

Another benefit of body percussion is that it gets the students playing immediately. There's no mini-lesson on mallet technique needed. Adding instruments later can then serve to heighten an already-rewarding experience.

Some body percussion sounds include stomps, claps, chest pats, tummy pats, thigh pats, snaps, and tongue clicks. Most percussion instruments can be easily substituted with a body percussion sound, such as stomping to produce a bass drum sound.

Found Objects

This can be a lot of fun. Have the students search for objects in the classroom that can produce cool percussion sounds. You could also invite the students to bring objects from home. A large cardboard box can serve as a great bass drum. Two pencils can be struck together as rhythm sticks. An empty five-gallon water bottle makes a fantastic hand drum. Make sure that all objects the students use, particularly recyclables, are clean!

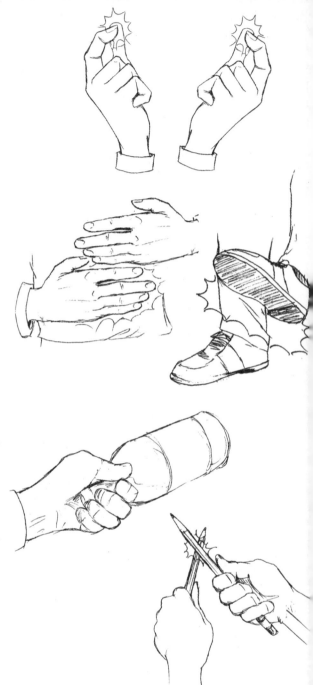

Orff Instruments

Find new uses for some old favorites. Students can take turns improvising melodies on the barred instruments while others play grooves on woodblocks, sand blocks, tambourines, triangles, etc. Students could also play in the groove on barred instruments, using one or two pitches.

Combine two or more of these ideas together

If you are in the process of building a collection of percussion instruments, but still don't have enough for every member of the circle, consider combining instruments with one of the options listed above. Try not to use the word "just," as in, "Students, if you don't have a percussion instrument, you can *just* use body percussion." Continue to emphasize the importance of the circle over what is played in that circle. And rotate a lot! After a groove has ended, have the students with instruments share those instruments with those who used body percussion or found objects.

But What Are They *Learning*?!

All this talk about facilitation over traditional teaching and musical experiences instead of musical performances may leave many of you asking, "It's great that the students are having a rewarding experience, but what are they *learning*?!" That's a fair question. How much time should your students spend playing drums when they still have to learn about melody, harmony, dynamics, composers, instruments, music of other world cultures, form, improvisation, etc.? Not to mention the holiday program, the spring concert, and all the other things that pop up.

To answer that, the following National Standards may be met in part, or in whole, by drum circle.

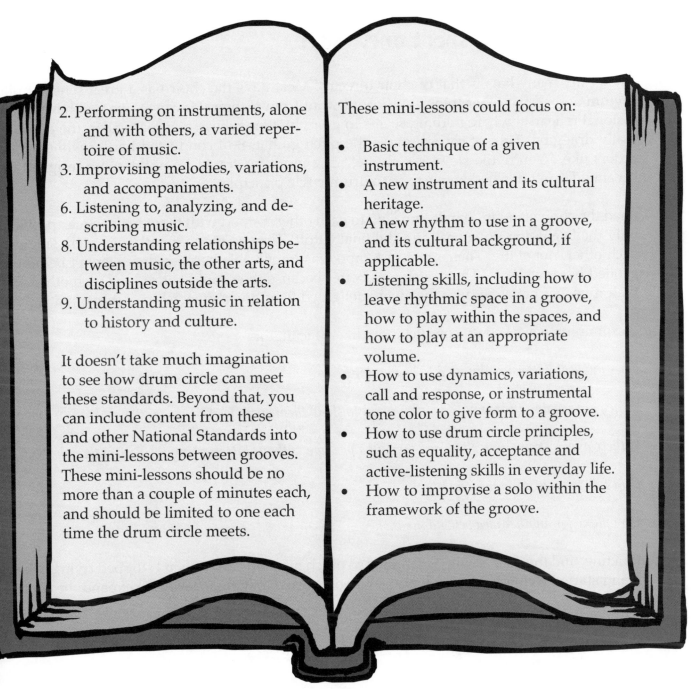

2. Performing on instruments, alone and with others, a varied repertoire of music.
3. Improvising melodies, variations, and accompaniments.
6. Listening to, analyzing, and describing music.
8. Understanding relationships between music, the other arts, and disciplines outside the arts.
9. Understanding music in relation to history and culture.

It doesn't take much imagination to see how drum circle can meet these standards. Beyond that, you can include content from these and other National Standards into the mini-lessons between grooves. These mini-lessons should be no more than a couple of minutes each, and should be limited to one each time the drum circle meets.

These mini-lessons could focus on:

- Basic technique of a given instrument.
- A new instrument and its cultural heritage.
- A new rhythm to use in a groove, and its cultural background, if applicable.
- Listening skills, including how to leave rhythmic space in a groove, how to play within the spaces, and how to play at an appropriate volume.
- How to use dynamics, variations, call and response, or instrumental tone color to give form to a groove.
- How to use drum circle principles, such as equality, acceptance and active-listening skills in everyday life.
- How to improvise a solo within the framework of the groove.

Trust your Music Teacher super powers! If it is something the students need to learn, the drum circle can probably teach it.

Expanding the Circle

I've mentioned some of the many things we each bring to the drum circle—our personalities, our different levels of rhythmic understanding, our joys, our concerns, our laughter, our need to express, our need to fit in. It's important to remember that all the valuable things we get from the circle can help us in our everyday lives. The circle doesn't have to stop at the door. Take the circle with you and encourage your students to do the same.

A true story (and a short one, too):

One of my many hats is that of choir director. Most days the choir has a great sense of pitch, rhythm and all the other things you could want from a choir. However, we will have that occasional rehearsal where nothing seems to go right. One rehearsal in particular, the choir was really dragging. This, of course, made the pitch go flat. So I conducted harder while barking orders like, "You're too slow! Watch me!" The more frustrated I got, the more resigned they became. Then it dawned on me to try a drum-circle principle.

I had the choir stand in a circle and sing to each other. I stood with them in the circle, providing only the beginning downbeat and the final cutoff. They sounded great! They were singing to each other, not at me. Their sense of tempo was impeccable because they weren't being bludgeoned by downbeats. Their pitch was better because they could better hear each other. Even their tone was better because they were delighted to be given ownership of the sound.

I started examining ways I could conduct more like a facilitator:

Does my beat pattern really need to be that big?

If they are keeping the tempo, do I even need to show them every beat?

Is there a way I can show them how to sing a passage without interrupting the flow of the rehearsal?

Do I talk too much in rehearsal?

Do I allow for another idea beyond my own?

My conducting, and the choir's singing, became so much more effective when I stopped trying to be the maestro and started trying to be a facilitator—when I started looking for ways to expand the circle.

Meet Mark Burrows

Mark Burrows received his undergraduate degree in music educa-tion from Southern Methodist University and his graduate degree in conducting from Texas Christian University. Mark is current-ly the Director of Fine Arts at First United Method Church – Fort Worth. He directs choral ensembles of all ages and oversees pro-grams in visual arts and theater. Prior to his work in Fort Worth, Mark was a music teacher at Stephen C. Foster Elementary School in Dallas, Texas.

Mark has written music and curriculum for numerous major pub-lishers. His song collections, including the *Gettin' Down with Mary Goose* series, top many best-seller lists. He also writes extensively for video, television and the stage.

Known to many little listeners as "Mister Mark," he tours national-ly, presenting high-energy family concerts. Mark's first CD, *You've Got a Song,* has won several awards for children's music.

Mark resides in Fort Worth, Texas with his wife Nina and daugh-ters Emma and Grace.

Two great companion books, also by Mark Burrows

The Body Electric

A Symphony of Sounds for Body Percussion (30/2181H)

Grades 2–6 • *The Body Electric* celebrates the music inside us while exploring ways to ex-press this music using the greatest instruments of all—our bodies. Part handy reference, part idea-generator, this collection is all fun as it introduces a self-contained instrumentar-ium that is convenient, inexpensive, physical, adaptable, self-affirming, educational, and, most of all, fun. An overview of and targeted examples for a variety of body, vocal and mouth sounds are included within the first two sections; great to teach the basics and to help student internalize rhythmic concepts. The last section includes songs that employ various combinations of all the introduced sounds. Reproducible student parts are includ-ed, as is a CD with helpful performance models of the sounds and pieces.

Planet Jams

An Exploration of the World's Rhythms and Percussion Instruments (30/2191H)

Grades 2–6 • Creating a world percussion resource for use in an elementary music setting is a lot like giving a world tour...from the space shuttle. The big picture is cool, but the de-tails seem to go zooming by faster than the speed of sound. Mark Burrows has embraced that challenge to craft this terrific collection, which includes units on West Africa, Brazil, Cuba, Spain, Middle East, India, Japan, North America and Samoa, as well as suggestions for making the most of the group percussion process. Each unit includes a brief overview of the geographical area; pictures and descriptions of several traditional percussion in-struments; basic techniques for playing those instruments and rhythms; and a process for teaching the music example. Reproducible student parts and a CD featuring authentic instruments are included to help facilitate the lessons, and Mark utilizes speech and body percussion throughout, making world percussion accessible to elementary general music classes.

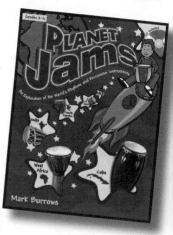